Do You Have All Your Parts?

My journey through the medical machinations of the human body.

Do You Have All Your Parts?

My journey through the medical machinations of the human body.

For information:
Janie Writes, a Small Press
1420 W. McDermott, #2016
Allen, Texas 75013

Janie's Email: janiewrites1@gmail.com
JanieWrites Website: https://janiewrites.weebly.com/

ISBN: 9798648630574

Imprint: Independently published by: JanieWrites
Printed in the United States of America
June 2020

Dedication

I would like to thank all the medical professionals I have interacted with over the years. Doctors, Nurse Practitioners, Nurses, EMTs, Paramedics, Ambulance Drivers, Aides, and any others I may have had reason to interact with during the 70 years since my birth. I would not be here if it were not for you.

Table of Contents

Foreword

In August 2019, I went to the ER with severe abdominal pain. I thought it was gas. I was wrong – almost dead wrong. After my ordeal, I noticed that most conversations among my peer group focused on illnesses, surgeries, and other medical machinations experienced. I decided I wanted to change the conversation.

The following pages are my personal story. They delineate my journey through various medical situations I have experienced. In no way do I wish to imply that I have had more serious or debilitating medical challenges than others have.

This is my story, some of it very personal and some of it I have never shared with anyone.

My purpose in writing this is simply to put it out there that we can be confronted by many kinds of challenges, yet we can prevail over them and still lead productive lives. While it is important to acknowledge our medical issues, we do not need focus on them or let them define our lives. They happened, sometimes they were hard, but we prevailed.

Our conversations can and should be about our accomplishments, our families, our lives, not what went wrong with those lives, but what went right.

I hope everyone reading this can relate in some way to some of the stories, and can take away from them a renewed sense of identity – one that is NOT based on "parts" but is based on who we are despite those parts.

Introduction

To look at me today, there is no way you can tell that I am missing "parts." I also have had "parts" replaced, "parts" repaired, "parts" injured and healed, additional "parts" added to my body, and "parts" changed from their original form. In fact, if you look around, chances are, many of the people you see every day do not possess 100% of their original "parts."

Dr. Christopher Cottrell, the surgeon who saved my life on August 30, 2019, chuckled, and related the interaction paraphrased below in response to my comment about being asked if I had all my "parts" during an incident in the ER. I said I did not want to be known by my "parts," or medical incidents, but rather by who I was to the people who knew me. A mother, a grandmother, a great-grandmother, a friend, and a writer.

This is what happened the Tuesday after Labor Day weekend, 2019 (artistic license taken, but the incident is true):

Dr. Cottrell and his colleague were doing exactly that – identifying me by my "parts." Of course, before that weekend, neither he nor his colleague in the Advanced Surgical of North Texas practice had ever seen me before. They did not know me by anything other than the complicated surgical procedure Dr. Cottrell performed on my small intestine the previous weeekend.

However, despite Dr. Cottrell's very intimate knowledge of parts of the inside of my body (he has held my intestines in his hands!) I still believe that we should get to know the people in our lives by things other than our "parts" and our medical circumstances.

Hundreds, indeed, thousands, of people have had their "parts" removed, injured, replaced, or repaired. Others were not born with all their parts. We hear stories every day about people overcoming their physical impairments, illnesses, and other shortcomings. I do not discount their stories, and I am in awe of them for their overcoming the limitations, but this book is about *my journey through the medical machinations of the human body*. I honestly believe that a positive attitude, coupled with amazing medical interventions, will help us through the most challenging situations.

Our bodies are simply miraculous. There is no other way to describe what the human body can do, what it can endure, and how it all works together.

This book is about miracles, plain and simple. It is not about the physical "how" of the inner workings of our bodies, it is about the fact that, despite all the damage we do to our bodies, whether on purpose or not, much of the time we can and do survive.

Most of us are born with all our parts intact. We have our arms, legs, feet, toes, hands, fingers, eyes, ears, etc. There are literally thousands of parts to the human body, and I cannot even begin to name them all here. There are parts visible to everyone, and parts that nobody ever sees. Or almost nobody.

Doctors and surgeons see parts of our bodies that we may never see. They replace, repair, or even remove parts. Sometimes they add in other parts when necessary.

During my visit to the hospital Emergency Room last fall, when I was suffering from acute abdominal pain, the doctors and nurses were having difficulty assessing what was wrong with me. One of the doctors turned away from the computer terminal he was standing at and asked me, "Do you have all your parts?"

"What?" I thought. "Um, no, I guess I don't" I replied. I then started to list my missing parts, a kidney, uterus, gall bladder. . . but the doctor had turned back to his computer terminal and I was not even sure I had answered him out loud. I was in extreme pain, under the influence of Morphine, and I was not sure about much of anything at that point.

Later I remembered the question, and that got me to thinking about my body parts – and what happened to them as I went through my life. So, I decided to write this book about all my "parts" and what happened to them, understanding that, even though my "parts" were compromised in different ways throughout my life, I am still a viable, productive, and healthy individual.

The majority of us who are born with all our parts intact rarely make it all the way through our lives with all those parts still intact. Some of us succumb to the disruption of our body parts – heart, kidney and other organ failure, accidents – lots of things take us away from our lives too early.

But some of us do make it to a ripe old age – whatever that means – despite our body parts trying to slow us down. I turned 70 years old shortly after the incident I mentioned above. Ever since that day in the ER when the doctor asked me whether or not I have all my parts, I have been thinking about my parts.

I'm going to take you on a journey through the medical machinations of my life – it has been filled with revision, removal, and replacement of my parts. But, as my surgeon so succinctly put it after the last episode, *"You're here!"* Yes, I'm here, and I feel just fine, despite missing several of my parts, and having other parts repaired or replaced.

One thing many people have said about me is that I am one of the most positive people they know. I have a positive outlook on life and circumstances. That attitude has, I believe, held me in good standing through some fairly harrowing experiences.

According to information I found on The Guardian Life Insurance website, *"Optimism is the practice of trying to look on the bright side when life gets dark. It's having faith that a positive outcome is just around the corner, and that there's no challenge in life too big for your strength.*

Although it's not always easy, consciously practicing optimism has proven to improve a person's quality of life in more ways than one." (Looking on the Bright Side: The Health Benefits of Positive Thinking, 2020)

I believe this. I have always been called a *Glass-Half-Full* kind of person, always finding the good in everything. I don't, as said above, have to practice optimism, I just am optimistic.

"Optimism can help your health by giving you the following:

- ***Improved coping abilities****: When faced with challenges, optimism can help you move past challenges without seeing them as a fault of your own. Instead, you can approach challenges as changeable, external to yourself, and not self-defining.*

- *Stronger immune system: Positivity can help fight disease and boost your immune system. In fact, optimism was found to be linked with a:*

  - *52% lower risk of dying from infection*

  - *16% lower risk of dying from cancer*

  - *38% lower risk of dying from heart disease*

  - *39% lower risk of dying from stroke*

  - *38% lower risk of dying from respiratory disease*

- *Better relationships: Studies reveal that when you are friends with an optimist, you can be impacted in a positive way. Simply put, happiness is contagious!*

But positive thinking doesn't come naturally for everyone." (Looking on the Bright Side: The Health Benefits of Positive Thinking, 2020)

Optimism does come naturally for me, and with this book I hope to show how that optimistic attitude helped me survive some fairly significant medical situations. That, and the fact that I want people to remember me as other than my parts – whether or not they have been removed, revised, or replaced.

Birth Stories

I want to start this missive with some stories that are unique to women. The human body, as I mentioned earlier, is an amazing miracle of parts – and women's bodies are even more unique in that they can reproduce.

The fact that a woman can grow another human inside her is amazing! I have been fortunate enough to give birth three times. A miscarriage early in my female maturity wasn't meant to be, and an ectopic pregnancy between my first and second child was obviously not part of the plan, but the three births I did accomplish produced three remarkable human beings.

I am starting this journey with those three birth stories because I want to show that the body can do wonderful things with its parts, just as it can do devasting things with those same parts.

Tim, Born June 27, 1968

My high school boyfriend joined the US Marine Corps shortly after he graduated. I was a senior the fall of 1967 when he was in boot camp. He came home on leave during the holidays and we made up for the time he was gone. By the time I went back to school in January 1968, I was pregnant, and Ron was on his way to Viet Nam.

In June, he was able to get an emergency leave and come home to marry me before our son was born. Tim was due around the middle of August. I had graduated from high school in early June via correspondence courses, so Ron and I decided to go to Glacier Park in Northern Montana on a honeymoon. We stopped at the courthouse in Helena, Montana, on June 26, 1968, and were married before a Justice of the Peace.

That night, six weeks before he was scheduled to arrive, our son, Tim, decided to make his entrance. Have you heard the phrase, "Honeymoon Baby?" Well, we have a *real* Honeymoon Baby!

I remember us finding the hospital in a strange town in the middle of the night, only to find the ER dark. We went around to the front of the hospital and walked up a very long flight of stairs. At the top of the stairs, the front door creaked open, and a little old man poked his head out. "Baby, huh?" he commented as he held the door open for us. He was the janitor/night watchman.

The hospital was very quiet as we made our way to the labor and delivery area. Tim was born in the early hours of June 27, 1968, weighing in at just over four pounds. He was so tiny, the oxygen mask they put on him covered his entire face. He had all his parts – but his lungs were compromised because of his unexpected early arrival. He was diagnosed with Hyaline Membrane disease, a common ailment in babies born prematurely.

Patrick Bouvier Kennedy, President John Kennedy's last child, was born three weeks early and died from Hyaline Membrane disease in 1963. The disease is also called Respiratory Distress Syndrome. I had heard about Hyaline Membrane but did not believe the doctors when they told me that my tiny baby would probably not survive longer than 72 hours because of it.

He was my baby, and he was going to be fine! I've always had an optimistic view of life and I believe that is the reason I survived so many medical events resulting in loss, revision, or replacement of my parts. Attitude is more than half the battle!

When he did survive, I was warned that he would likely be small for his age, possibly suffer some kind of brain damage due to the lack of oxygen at birth, and not to expect much.

My son will celebrate his 52nd birthday this year, he is over six feet tall, played football in high school, was on the honor roll, and an officer in his class. He served in the Army, and now lives in Germany, where he speaks fluent German and works as a delivery driver for DHL. He has three children and is expecting his fourth grandchild in the fall of 2020.

I guess they didn't know everything about premature babies in 1968.

Roni, Born April 27. 1970

In 1970 our second child was born. Because the first time I gave birth resulted in a 6-week preemie, I was unprepared for a full-term birth. I knew nothing about Braxton-Hicks contractions, and a week before she was actually born, Ron and I rushed to the Naval Hospital at Camp Pendleton, California. I was having what I thought were premature contractions again.

Ron had been transferred to Camp Pendleton with the Marine Corps from North Las Vegas, where his first post-Viet Nam assignment was.

I was a little skeptical of the care I would receive at the Naval Hospital as I had recently had a bad experience there. I had gone for a regularly scheduled pre-natal visit a month or so before my baby was due. They put me in a curtained cubicle near the back of the large room to wait for the doctor. There were probably 10 cubicles in the room, maybe more. It was a very large hospital. I was decked out in a gown tied in the back, and nothing else, waiting on the bed when the lights in the building went out.

The only sound I heard was the door at the end of the room closing. I opened the curtain to see if I could figure out what was going on, and I saw…nothing. Everyone was gone. The clock on the wall, illuminated from the back, showed a few minutes after 5:00. Evidently, they had closed up and gone home, forgetting that I was still there!

So, you can understand my hesitation when I went to the Labor and Delivery section of the same hospital in mid-April 1970, thinking I was in labor. Back then fathers were considered unnecessary in labor rooms, so they checked me in and sent Ron home, only to call him an hour later to come and get me. I had been experiencing false labor.

When it was finally time for Roni, our daughter, to arrive, off we went to the hospital again. Ron was sent home again and I was placed in a bed in the labor room. My contractions were coming fast and hard, but the nurses said I couldn't have the baby yet. The doctor wasn't there.

The baby didn't seem to care about the doctor's presence. She was coming and there was no stopping her. I remember one nurse telling me to cross my legs, that the doctor wasn't there yet, and I was not to have that baby until he arrived.

A few minutes later, that same nurse 'caught' my baby girl. Roni was born in the labor room without the assistance of the doctor. When he finally arrived, I was on a bed in the hallway, waiting transportation to a room. The nurses had

the baby and were doing what they do with new babies –
cleaning her up and getting her ready for me.

The doctor, gloves and mask on, stopped at my bed and
patted me absently on the head. "You did fine." He said.

"So did you," I replied, somewhat sarcastically.

Amy, Born April 10, 1973

By the time our third child was born, Ron was out of the military and we were back in Billings, Montana. We had purchased our first home in the West end of town and Ron was working in the family travel business.

I had expressed my desire to have this baby at home, but my Obstetrician was against it. He said it wasn't safe. When I went into labor, I reluctantly went to the hospital, where they promptly sent my husband home. Again, fathers were not welcome at the birth of their children back then.

Interestingly enough, though, they allowed my mother to stay with me during the early part of my labor confinement. She told me later how the nurses kept trying to keep me quiet. Apparently, I was yelling too loud and was disturbing other laboring moms. I don't remember that.

I do remember, however, insisting that I be allowed to leave the hospital hours after Amy was born. The nurses said I couldn't go, but when they saw I was determined to leave, they said I couldn't take the baby with me.

I didn't listen to them. Amy was my baby, and I was taking her with me. They couldn't stop me. I did, however, agree to bring her back when she was three days old for her PKU test. The PKU test is a newborn screening test that looks for evidence of a genetic disorder that can possibly lead to seizures, behavioral problems, and mental disorders.

So, while I did not have the baby at home, I did not stay in the hospital after she was born. We spent her first night at home, just where I wanted to be.

All three of my children are healthy, thriving adults now. Each of them has children and grandchildren of their own. So, because my body's parts were able to create and grow three humans, there are now 18 (soon to be 19) more humans on the earth: my children, grandchildren, and great-grandchildren.

Of course, this did not start with me, there was my mom, grandmother, and countless other women in my past that started this phenomenon. In fact, my great great grandmother, Elizabeth Jarvis, was born on November 24, 1849, exactly one hundred years before my birthday. But that's another story for another time. Women and their parts are obviously essential to the furtherance of the human race.

When Things go South

Things don't always stay the same. Our parts are constantly growing, changing, and developing. Sometimes there are problems. Sometimes we do things to our parts, causing them to malfunction. Sometimes it is our bodies that rebel and cause parts to fail.

Medical advances are getting better all the time, but the doctors can't always fix the parts. Medications are often the first line of defense after lifestyle choices regarding diet and exercise don't work or cause problems.

When medications fail or are not appropriate, the surgeons can step in. I have had more than my share of interactions with surgeons, both because of my lifestyle choices and because my body caused problems for itself.

Following is an account of the surgeries I have had, and the scars that resulted from those surgeries. As you read this, keep in mind that these are accounts of parts going bad, needing repair, removal, or replacement. They are just parts – They are not how I define myself. I like to think I am more than my parts.

It is essential, however, that you understand that, although I don't define myself in terms of my parts, the removal, repair, or replacement of those parts has defined my life in certain ways. I have been able to survive and live a full life even though my parts have malfunctioned, been replaced, removed, or revised.

Surgeries

I have had surgery multiple times, sometimes it was a simple procedure, done on an out-patient basis, other times I spent several days in the hospital. Surgery is often used as a last resort after other treatments of certain medical situations have been exhausted.

For example, I have torn rotator cuffs in both of my shoulders, causing pain, difficulty in lifting heavy objects, or just moving my arm in a certain direction. I have had both shoulders x-rayed, and have been advised by the orthopedic surgeon that surgery is an option.

Key word here: option. I have chosen at this time to not go under the knife, but instead to manage with physical therapy and pain medication if needed. So far, so good. I have learned to live with the discomfort, I try not to do a lot of heavy lifting, and I do have a supply of Tylenol handy if needed.

There are other times and situations, however, that require surgery. With both my knees, the situation was so severe that no amount of physical therapy would change it, and when I had a necrotic bowel situation surgery saved my life. Surgery should not be a frivolous choice, but one taken if there are no other options, or after all else has failed.

The following stories relate my experience with surgeons and surgery. I have the scars to show I went under the knife multiple times.

My Body is a Road Map

The surgical scars on my body resemble a road map with lines going every which way. There's that long one that starts in the middle of my back, stretches around my right side and points down to below my ribcage. Lost a kidney through that one. My son said I looked like I was the person in a magic show that got cut in half by a magician who didn't know what he was doing!

There's a bit of a multi-purpose scar from just below my belly button and runs about three inches down. The first time that area of my body was cut into was to remove a portion of my fallopian tube because an embryo had started to grow outside the womb and attached to the wall of my tube.

After my third child was born, the doctors used that scar to remove my uterus, followed years later by serving as the end of a 16-inch scar starting just below my breastbone. That one required 40 staples to hold it together after the doctor removed eight feet of my small intestine through it. It takes a funny little jog around my belly button.

When I joked with the surgeon about it not being a straight line, he replied, "You're not straight! You have so much loose skin on your belly it wasn't easy trying to make a straight line." More about that loose skin later.

Each of my knees sport two scars, each one about three inches long where the torn cartilage was removed, creating a bone-on-bone situation which would cause problems years later. Both knees have since been replaced, leaving ten-inch scars on the sides of each knee.

There are numerous small scars, insertion points for laparoscopic surgeries, where the doctor sticks long needles or other instruments through little, quarter inch incisions and looks around inside through tiny cameras. My gall bladder left through one of those little scars.

I even have scars on my toes! Hammer toe and neuroma removal in my left foot made it easier to walk and put on shoes. There's a pin in the second toe on my right foot, keeping it straight.

The scar from carpal tunnel surgery in my right hand is barely visible, as is the scar on my right wrist where the doctor removed a book cyst.

There are scars on the front of each shoulder – one to close up the incision where my pacemaker was installed, and one where the IV port was inserted for cancer treatment (chemotherapy) access.

I have had basil cell carcinomas removed from my right cheek, the left side of my nose, the back of my neck, my abdomen, and just under my right eye. There appears to be another of these pesky skin cancers growing on my lower right eyelid and on the tip of my left ear. I have had four large bumpy cysts removed from my head. Those scars don't show under my hair. My dermatologist said I was one of the "lucky ones!" Apparently, I am "really good" at growing cysts and basil cell cancers. Ha!

I'm sure there are more, but the point is, those scars are badges of survival. The marks on my skin serve to prove that I endured something, but came out of whatever it was with just a line of raised, sometimes pink, mostly faded tissue as a reminder of what happened.

The following pages contain an account of how those scars occurred. I'll try to go in chronological order, but bear with me if I skip ahead occasionally.

Tonsillectomy

I was a kid, like most people who undergo a tonsillectomy are, when my parents opted to have me go under the knife for the first time. I was in high school, maybe a junior, I'm not sure. I don't remember much about it, other than my disappointment when I recovered and was told I could NOT have all the ice cream I wanted!

That's what everybody said about getting your tonsils out – I could have ice cream for every meal if I wanted! I think that's why I agreed to do it. I do remember that the surgery took place in the doctor's office, with me sitting up in a chair.

When the doctor said I could not have any ice cream, I was upset. He explained that dairy products caused phlegm to build up in the throat, and that was not good for my recovery. What a disappointment! After all that, and I couldn't even have ice cream.

This was my first experience with having one of my parts removed. Evidently tonsils are not required for one to have a regular, healthy life. In the 50-plus years since that happened, I believe I can count on one hand the number of colds and/or sore throats I have had. So, that begs the question, "Why have tonsils in the first place?"

There is no obvious scar from the tonsillectomy, and even if there is one, nobody can see it unless they are looking down my throat with some kind of scope or light.

Ectopic Pregnancy

A few years later, after the birth of my first child, I experienced something that dropped me to my knees. My husband, who was a Marine, and I were living in Las Vegas while he was stationed as an MP at Nellis Air Force Base.

I was hanging clothes on the line, my toddler son playing in the grass at my feet, when I experienced a series of very sharp pains in my abdomen. Severe abdominal pain would become something of a mantra in my life over the next several years, but I didn't know that at the time.

I ended up in the base hospital, with the first of what would be several abdominal surgeries throughout my life. I was diagnosed with an ectopic pregnancy, one where the fertilized embryo attaches itself to a part it shouldn't be attached to and starts to grow and develop.

In my case, the embryo had gotten stuck in the fallopian tube on its way to my uterus. There is not enough room to grow in a fallopian tube, so as the embryo began its natural process of developing and growing, it caused extreme pain, again in my abdomen.

Six weeks after surgery to remove my fallopian tube and the ill-fated embryo, I was in the doctor's office for a check-up. He completed his exam, and stated, "I'm sure we discussed the idea that you should not become pregnant again so soon after this surgery."

My somewhat sheepish response was, "But you didn't say anything about that to my husband." Eight months later, our second child was born.

Surgical Tube Tying

At some point after our third child was born, my husband decided he had other priorities more important than raising a family. He left the four of us to pursue those priorities. To be completely fair, we were both very young when we got married and the birth of our first child on our honeymoon didn't help.

One thing I was sure about at this time was I did not want to have any more children. I was 25 years old, single, and the mother of three kids, all under seven years old. I wanted to get my fallopian tubes tied because I knew I would likely marry again, and did not want the issue of more children to even be an option.

You may think that was selfish of me, but I knew I was not prepared to have another baby or raise another child.

I only had one tube, having lost the other one in the ectopic pregnancy, however there was no impact on my fertility because of having only one tube. I had given birth twice since having it removed. I explained all this to my doctor, who still refused to do the surgery. He said I was too young, and would eventually marry again and WANT more children. Funny how he thought he knew what I wanted. He obviously didn't live in my body, nor in my life at the time. I was determined to get my remaining tube tied as I knew for sure that birthing another child was not to be in my future.

I saw a couple other doctors, who told me the same thing. I finally found one who agreed with me and consented to the surgery. I had my second tube tied through a laparoscopic incision in my belly button. The next day I looked like I had been kicked in the belly with a sharp-toed cowboy boot. The bruising eventually faded and there was no discernable scar. So, I lost a part because of the ectopic pregnancy, and had its matching part altered through surgical tube tying.

I would have no more children, but I sported a new scar just below my belly button from the ectopic pregnancy. The one in my belly button from the tube tying did not show.

Hysterectomy

As it turned out, I didn't need to have the tube tied in order to prevent any future pregnancies. About a year after that procedure, in 1975, my brother found me lying on the floor of the radio studio at the college I was attending. I was the evening DJ as part of my studies toward a degree in Journalism.

My brother wanted to watch me work, so had stopped by the studio, only to find me curled up in pain on the floor. More abdominal pain. The building was empty as it was after regular day classes had ended and the night classes were not in session yet. The studio was a small FM station on campus with a limited broadcast area.

We shut off the equipment and went to the hospital ER. My regular OB met me there and had me sent directly to the operating room for a hysterectomy. I had developed fibroid tumors and endometriosis, which were causing extreme pain. Back in the early 70s the recommended treatment for both conditions was a full hysterectomy.

Just before they put me out, the doctor asked me if I was planning on wearing a bikini in the future. I thought it was a rather odd question at the time, but I said, "No."

Later when I asked him why he asked about the bikini, he explained that if I was planning on wearing a bikini, he would do a horizontal incision across the bottom of my abdomen to do the hysterectomy. Since I was not planning on bikini wearing, he went ahead and did a vertical incision, actually opening the previous scar from the ectopic pregnancy.

He explained that the vertical incision took less time in the operating room, thus costing less. It would also heal faster. A horizontal incision would mean cutting across the abdominal muscles, taking longer in the OR, which charged by the minute, making a horizontal incision more expensive. Something the insurance company might frown upon. The vertical incision simply went between the muscles, which enabled the surgeon to sew me up quicker.

This incision was my first experience with surgical staples, a more efficient method of closing wounds. A couple weeks later the staples came out and my new incision healed quickly.

Cartilage Removal, both knees

One winter in the late 80s, I went to Arizona to visit my parents, who were spending the winter in the desert. The kids were all pretty small, and we were getting along as a single parent family quite nicely. I had moved from Billings, Montana to Missoula, Montana to attend the Journalism school at the University of Montana and we decided a trip to warm Arizona was in order during the holidays. Someone laughingly called us "Snow Chicks." My parents were called "Snowbirds," that designation given to the thousands of elderly people who made the annual pilgrimage to the southern deserts from the frozen mountains in Montana and other northern states.

We were enjoying the warm weather at a picnic with the family at Saguaro Lake, near Phoenix, when I decided it would be fun to play with a frisbee. Throwing and catching it across the picnic ground was fun, at least until I twisted just the wrong way and tore the cartilage in both knees. I returned to Montana in a wheelchair, both knees swollen and wrapped in ace bandages.

As it was a winter vacation, I had a bit of fun telling my friends back home that it was a skiing accident, which seemed more exciting than what really happened. I mean, who wrecked their knees catching a frisbee? Anyhow, I saw an orthopedic surgeon soon after my return to Montana, who recommended surgery. Keep in mind, this was in the early 80s, and the recommended course of action for torn knee cartilage was removal.

Each of my knees has a 3-inch scar along the side, evidence of the cartilage removal surgery. It was years before I experienced problems with my knees again. The first thing the orthopedic surgeon asked years later was, "You had your cartilage removed about 20 years ago, didn't you?" When I responded positively, he added, "We don't do that anymore."

You can read what happened in the chapter titled "Replaced Parts."

Right Nephrectomy

In 1985 I was living in rural Montana with my three children. One morning I noticed that I was peeing what appeared to be pure blood. I had no pain, and knew it was not because of my period as I had undergone a hysterectomy about ten years before.

The only medical option to me at that time was a local clinic staffed by a nurse. There was no doctor available in our small town, but I didn't think there was anything seriously wrong enough to warrant a trip 50 miles to the nearest city.

The nurse confirmed that there was an inordinate amount of blood in my urine and encouraged me to make the trip to the city to see a urologist.

After several visits and tests, a CT scan was ordered. The urologist told me that the scan showed a growth on my right kidney. It was near the opening to the ureter and his recommendation was surgery.

Once again, I checked in to the hospital for abdominal surgery – this time in the lower right quadrant toward the back of my abdomen.

After I recovered from the surgery, the doctor explained that when they opened me up, they saw the growth on my kidney. He said he it was dark colored and when he touched it, it would blanche – or turn white, then fill with fluid again and resume the dark color. That told him that it was a fluid-filled growth, but he was not sure what the fluid was. His fear was that it was cancerous, and if he cut it to remove it, it would leak and spread cancer cells in the area.

"I have good news, and I have bad news." He said.

After he removed my entire kidney, they tested the growth on it. The good news was that the growth was a cyst, and not cancerous. The bad news was that, if they had known that, they would not have taken my kidney out. It was too late by then, however. My kidney had been dissected in pathology and could not be returned.

He assured me that a person could live a normal life with only one kidney. He did caution me about future activities, however. He said I should not rappel off a mountain, go bungee jumping, ride a motocross cycle, or any other life-threatening activities. Since I had never done any of those things, I suppose I could have been disappointed that I never would be able to, but I thought, "Oh well. Avoiding those activities was going to be easy!"

Now, some forty years after losing my kidney, I have experienced some issues, but nothing serious or life changing. I just have to watch my intake of pain medicine like NSAIDS like Ibuprofen (Advil, Motrin) and Naproxen (Aleve). The only pain killer I can safely take is Tylenol.

My last ultrasound showed two cysts on my left kidney, very similar to the one that was on my right kidney, but the nephrologist said there was no reason to worry about them – unless they grow quickly. We check on them once a year or so, and so far, there has been no change in them. I lost my right kidney – and the left is compromised, but I'm fine and feel no effects from the changes in these two parts. Most of the time, I don't even think about them.

Duodenal Switch Weight Loss

This is chapter is not easy to write. I made lifestyle choices that resulted in me damaging portions of my body. I gained weight, as do a lot of people, but my weight was out of control.

When I attended my oldest granddaughter's destination wedding in Jamaica in June 2015, I had been reduced to using a walker because I was so heavy, and my left knee was so bad I could not walk unassisted. I look back on photos from the wedding and I am embarrassed, and somewhat shocked at how I looked. By that time, I was near 350 lbs.

I sold my home in Arizona in early 2016 and moved to Texas to be near my oldest daughter and her family. I knew I needed to have my knee replaced, but no doctor would do the surgery because of my extreme weight.

I almost gave up. I decided that I was just destined to be fat and crippled the rest of my life. I started to define myself by my "parts." My body was huge, my knee was very painful, and I felt I was out of options.

At the time I was working for an online training company, doing corporate training at home from my computer. In the past, I had traveled for the company, doing the training in person, but had stopped traveling because of my weight. It was just too hard to get around in airports.

When I flew, I used a wheelchair at the airport, had to ask for a seatbelt extender because the regular seatbelt did not go around me. I squeezed into the seat, and am sure the passenger sitting next to me was as uncomfortable as I was. I did not fit, part of my bulk flowed into the seat next to me.

I always tried to take an aisle seat because I did not want to have to squeeze past my seatmates if I had to get up during the flight. It was a terrible situation, and one I gladly gave up when I told the training company I could not do on-site training anymore. Plus, I was ashamed to be in front of people in my condition.

I had fallen several times because of my knee, and was using a walker. A clarifying moment came to me one day at the pool at my senior apartment complex in Texas. I had signed up for a water aerobics class, believing deep inside that it wouldn't help, but I was trying to convince myself that I was making changes.

I was sitting in my walker after the class that day when the walker collapsed. My weight was just too much for it and the legs gave out. I could not stand up by myself (*Help, I've fallen, and can't get up!* has real meaning for me.) The women in the class were all older than me and could not help.

They called 911 and the paramedics came to lift me to my feet and walk me to my apartment. Although I laughed and joked about the "hot" firemen rescuing me, I was devastated inside. I never went back to the water aerobics class.

During this time, I had been working with an editing client, Dr. Audrey Pullman. Audrey is a Performance Enhancement Specialist with a background in Emergency Psychiatric Medicine and Community Addiction. She has written a series of books under the heading *Your Unique Style*. Volume I is called *I Want My Body Back*, Volume II is *Your Unique Style of Fit*, and Volume III is *Self Esteem and Your Unique Style of Fit*. All three books deal with body image, weight loss, and mindset.

I edited and published the books for Audrey and over the years we have become friends. As I was editing her manuscripts, I was able to identify with the issues she was writing about. One of my biggest take-aways from the series is this statement by Audrey in the first book: *First, all humans have their own uniqueness and genetic makeup so to lose weight isn't one size fits all.* (Pullman, I Want My Body Back, 2018)

Because of what Audrey wrote, and what the orthopedic surgeons were saying about my weight and replacing my knee, I decided to see a weight loss specialist to determine if there was anything I could do about my weight. By that time, I was topping the scale 365 pounds.

Dr. Ayoola, of the Weight Loss Specialists of North Texas assured me that there was something I could do. Weight loss surgery. I was hesitant to go that route because I knew some people would not understand, would think I took the easy way out, etc. I remember once when I was with a group of the older women at the retirement complex where I lived, I said something about weight, and the response from one very tall, very thin woman was "Just eat less."

It's not that easy, and I decided if I did have the surgery, I would not tell anyone. I went ahead and scheduled the surgery for the end of March 2017. It was a difficult recovery, I was sick for weeks after, and have had issues eating since then.

I cannot eat large meals as the surgery, called "Duodenal Switch" re-arranged parts in my abdomen, cutting off access to much of my stomach, among other revisions of the many parts involved in eating and the processing of food.

It is now nearly three years later, and I have lost over 200 lbs. I feel much better, I am mobile, I have not used a walker in a long time, I had my left knee replaced, and I fit in airplane seats now!

I am now at my ideal weight, I try to eat healthy, protein rich food, and do lots of walking. I am also starting up a water aerobics class again. This time I won't be using a walker to get to the pool!

There is another consequence of losing a significant amount of weight, however. I now feel like I am wearing a skin suit that is 15 sizes too big! I do have lots of extra skin, all over, and it does make me a bit self-conscious at times.

When I was at my heaviest, I wore a size 26 and now I have trouble keeping my size 12 jeans from sliding off my almost non-existent hips! My most recent purchase was a pair of size 10 capri pants. And, I could probably fly with the flaps of skin hanging off my arms. My granddaughter calls them my wings!

My health insurance won't cover cosmetic surgery, and skin removal surgery will cost thousands of dollars. I will learn to live with it. Remember earlier I mentioned the abdominal scar that I teased my surgeon about it not being straight? The loose skin on my abdomen is why. He did jog around my belly button, but the loose skin on my tummy made it hard to cut the rest of the incision in a straight line.

An interesting side-effect of being so big, one that I did not realize while I was logging in the pounds, was invisibility. Yes, as big as I was, I was apparently invisible. People seemed to look right through me, or if they saw me at all they looked at me with disgust. At least, that's what I thought.

After I lost the weight, I noticed that people would talk to me. Just random conversations with strangers at the grocery store, or out with my family.

I was surprised the first few times this happened, then I realized that, for years, I would go through my life being completely ignored by strangers. I do not remember a stranger ever saying anything to me at a store or restaurant. Even when flying, my seatmates never spoke to me.

A couple months ago I flew back to Arizona for a visit and found myself in nice conversations with people in the airport, on the plane, even standing in line at the car rental counter. This NEVER happened when I was fat. Did you know fat people were invisible?

Not surprisingly, one comment I heard after I lost all the weight was, "…and she did it the right way – didn't take a short cut like surgery." I have never told that person that I did have the surgery, but it was not an easy way out at all. The recovery was harder than I ever expected, and to this day I still have some issues related to eating.

I like to go back to my friend Audrey's statement about the law of attraction: *The law of attraction is the manifestation of your thoughts. When you understand everything in existence is made up of the same core ingredients of tiny vibrating energy particles you will gain knowledge of how people attract the events that happen in their lives.* (Pullman, Self Esteem and Your Unique Style, 2018)

Gall Bladder

I remember when my mom had to have an emergency surgery to remove her gall bladder, she told me that there were three factors that compounded gall bladder problems: *Female*, *Fat*, and *Forty*.

I'll never forget that, so when my weight loss doctor said, as a precautionary step in the weight loss process through surgery, they often removed the gall bladder, I was not surprised. He said that in most cases, within six months of this kind of surgery, patients often presented with gall bladder issues and had to have it removed.

I was *Female*, and *Fat*, but I was 20 years past my *Forties* by that time. I agreed to have my gall bladder removed. Dr. Ayoola took it out through one of the multiple laparoscopic incisions used during the weight loss surgery.

Several of the eating and digestion problems I experienced after the surgery were because of the gall bladder surgery. I have to avoid eating fatty foods like chips and pastries. Of course, not eating those foods also helps with the weight loss.

After duodenal switch surgery, I also have to avoid eating lots of carbohydrates and should eat lots of protein. All the same advice given to people on regular diets. The difference is, if I eat things like excess fatty foods or carbohydrates, I will suffer multiple gastric consequences.

I have a lot of scar tissue in my abdomen as a result of the multiple surgeries: the kidney, gall bladder, uterus, fallopian tubes, the weight loss surgery, all left scar tissue, which later turned out to cause some other issues. Read about that in the next section.

Necrotic Bowel

Of all my surgeries, some of which I have not even gotten to yet in this recounting, this one is probably the most significant. At least from everyone else's point of view. According to something I read online, surgery to remove a large portion of the small bowel is the second most serious surgery performed in the US. It has a mortality rate of 6.5%, and costs start at around $23,000 for the surgery alone.

I still have problems reconciling what happened with how I feel today.

I woke up at around 2:00 AM on the morning of August 30, 2019. I had a belly ache. I had been going through some of those gastric episodes I mentioned after my weight loss surgery and initially dismissed this as a bad case of gas.

It was very painful, and would come and go in waves. Sometimes hurting a lot, then waning to almost nothing before starting up again. I told myself that if it didn't get better by 3:00 AM, I would call my daughter, Roni, and let her know something was wrong. Then I would call 911.

I also knew, however, that Roni was planning on going to Chicago later that morning and I didn't want to interrupt her plan to visit my granddaughter, Chloe, who was going to school at Loyola University. I finally called 911 about 2:45 AM. I was in a great deal of pain and I knew something was wrong.

I tried to call Roni from the ambulance, but she didn't answer – she was asleep and didn't hear the phone ring. I left her a couple messages. In the meantime, the paramedic in the ambulance could not get an IV started. He was having problems finding a vein.

The next several hours are a blur. I have images swirling in my mind of lots of people coming in and out of the ER. I know I was given more than one dose of Morphine for pain, but the pain just kept getting worse. I remember having doctors, nurses, and other medical people in the room, poking at my arms and legs with needles, trying to find a vein.

My granddaughter, Darrah, who is a registered nurse, was in the room with me. I wasn't sure how she came to be there, but later my daughter told me she called her in because she was going to Chicago and didn't want to leave me alone. I do remember seeing my daughter briefly, evidently just before she left for the airport.

It was confusing, but there are a few clear moments I can recall. One was when I turned to Darrah and asked her if it was snowing in the room. I remember that I thought I was looking out the window at a blue mailbox and it was snowing, both inside and outside. This was more than likely a Morphine-induced hallucination. I also remember seeing a doctor standing near the foot of my bed at a computer terminal. He turned and asked me if I had all my parts. I'm pretty sure that happened.

Another clear memory I have is one of a lot of people in the room, medical people as well as just regular people. One was an older woman wearing a red turban. She got right in my face, smiled, and said everything was going to be all right. Now of course, these memories are all fueled by Morphine, so I can't say for sure that they are accurate.

The last image I have of that morning was the clock on the wall as they wheeled me into the operating room.

I wrote a short story about what I think was a near-death experience during those few hours in the ER and operating room. I'm including it here, even though some of the experiences have already been told part of the larger story. It was very real to me, although there is some question as to who a lot of the people I mention actually existed. The whole idea of a near-death experience is fascinating to me. I'm not sure I believed in near-death experiences until it happened to me.

I originally wrote the story for a book compiled by a good friend of mine, Dr. Sheila Embry. She is putting together an anthology of what she calls "angel stories," stories by friends of hers who have experienced situations where there surely was a guardian angel or two watching over them. The book, working title, *"At the Right Time"* will be coming out in late June 2020. You can find information about it and Sheila's other books at her Amazon Author page: https://www.amazon.com/Sheila-Embry/e/B003HWM3PI (Embry, 2020)

My inclusion of this story is simply for thought and possibly discussion.

The Red Turban

My memories of the early morning on August 30, 2019 are convoluted, hazy, and somewhat confusing. I know I was in the ER. There were lots of people around, nurses, medial techs, doctors. I remember being poked at and prodded several places. My arms, my legs, my groin area. I couldn't move, waves of pain kept washing over me, sometimes so strong I couldn't breathe. I thought I might be in labor, but that was impossible. I had a hysterectomy over 40 years before, but it felt like labor.

I remember seeing my granddaughter, Darrah's face as she peered at me. "Grandma, I'm here." Someone took my earrings and rings off – handed them to Darrah.

The nurses kept saying things like, "I can't get a pulse." Or "I can't find a vein." Or, "Go get so-and-so, he's really good at finding veins." People swirled around, I thought it was snowing in the room at one point. I asked the nurse to just put me to sleep so I wouldn't feel the pain.

The gurney I was on was rolled out into the hallway. People following, holding up tubes and charts. It was confusing. The lights in the ceiling flashed in my eyes so I closed them. They asked me to move to another table for a CT scan, but I couldn't move. I tried, rolled over in between the gurney and the CT table, but couldn't get any further. I giggled. "I'm done. That's as far as I go." The morphine was kicking in.

In the hallway again, lights flashing by on the ceiling. The last thing I remember seeing was the clock on the wall as they pushed the gurney through a set of double doors. 12:00. Was that noon or midnight? It must be noon. I remember calling 911 at 3:00am. It couldn't be midnight. After that, there was nothing.

Not until later, I don't know how much later, but there were lots of people in the room again. Medical people in scrubs and white coats, but others, too. Just regular people in regular clothes. Milling around. Some of them looked at me, but most of them just wandered around the room, looking at the medical people. Then one face came really close to mine. She grinned. A bright red turban covered her head, but I imagined grey hair under it. Her pale face was soft and wrinkled. Her eyes were sharp and flashing, or maybe shining.

She smiled at me. I felt calm and very peaceful, despite the confusion all around me. There were so many people in the room! The woman in the turban came closer, smiling widely all the way. When she was almost nose-to-nose with me, she said, "It's going to be all right now."

Later the doctor told me he was about to start CPR in the operating room when I seemed to settle down. He proceeded with the surgery to remove eight feet of necrotic bowel from my small intestine. He told my granddaughter, waiting outside the OR, that I had "coded" twice on the operating table, but I was stable now. He told her I had about a 50-50 chance of surviving. His biggest worry was sepsis, an often-fatal infection arising from something like this.

I am fine now; I have a scar running from just below my breastbone to two inches below my navel. It takes a bit of a jog around the belly button, and ends at the top of the tattooed blue dot placed there the year before as a marker for the radiologist who used it to locate the right place to aim the radiology machine for the cancer treatment I completed in 2018. I now have a 16-inch exclamation point on my belly!

The woman in the red turban. Who was she? My angel? My Crone Guide? A figment of my morphine-filled mind? I choose to believe she was real. She was letting me know I would survive, and everything would be fine. She was right. It has been nine months since that time in the ER and I do not feel any different than I did before – except I know I am alive when many involved that day did not think I would be.

~End~

I was suffering from a Necrotic Bowel. *"Necrotic bowel is a condition characterized by the death of gastrointestinal tissue,"* explained Dr. Christopher Cottrell, the surgeon called in for the emergency situation. *"In Janie's case, a portion of her intestine had lost its blood supply because of a prior surgery and a resulting internal hernia. The sepsis it caused is life-ending without expedient surgery."* (Biggs, 2020)

According to Michelle Biggs, blogger for the North Texas Health Resources, who interviewed both me and Dr. Cottrell for a blog post published on the Health resources website, *"The surgery was complicated, requiring Cottrell to remove the most obvious site of necrosis in the bowel. To accomplish this, he had to define the anatomy and remove extensive scar tissue from prior surgeries. Once an internal road map was identified, the bowel could safely be removed. However, when the initial surgical site began to show additional signs of tissue death, Dr. Cottrell had to again remove bowel to prevent sepsis.* (Biggs, 2020)

After surgery, I was transferred to the Post-Anesthesia Care Unit (PACU) with, as told to my waiting granddaughter, Darrah, and friend, Irene, about a 50-50 chance of survival.

Sometime later, I was surprised to see my daughter, Amy, who lived in Arizona, walk into my room in the PACU. I didn't understand why she was there. Over the next several hours my family and the medical staff filled me in on the events that preceded my stay in the PACU.

Evidently there was a lot of discussion and frantic speculation about what was going on with me. In the end, they called in Dr. Cottrell, who discovered that my small intestine was dying, He was a specialist in this kind of situation, and I do believe he saved my life. In the OR, he removed over eight feet of my small intestine.

Prior to the surgery, he called my daughter, Roni, who had arrived in Chicago, and asked if I had a DNR (Do Not Resuscitate) order. That is apparently when she called her sister in Arizona and decided to get her on a plane to Texas. She also flew back to Texas, leaving her husband in Chicago with their daughter.

My son in Germany was waiting to hear something, ready to get on a plane as well. By the time Roni got back from Chicago and Amy was here from Texas, I had come through surgery and survived. Tim in Germany decided to come visit a few weeks later.

I mentioned that I was still having problems reconciling what happened with how I feel. I know it was a serious situation, everyone involved has told me several times that I almost died during the procedure. I find this hard to believe as I feel just fine and could not imagine something so serious taking place.

Even the doctor was surprised to see me alive and well a few days later. Here is my dilemma: I feel just fine. I don't feel any different than I did before that night. The only way I know for sure it even happened is when I see the 16-inch scar running down my belly.

At times I even feel a bit guilty for causing so much turmoil for my family and friends. I think it goes back to what I have said before: I do not want to be defined by my parts, or lack of parts, in this case. I am not the lady with the intestine.

I am a mother, a grandmother, a great-grandmother, a friend, and a writer.

Replaced Parts

Sometimes the parts we are born with stop working correctly and surgery is required to fix them. Sometimes they are simply removed like the ones I mentioned above. I am missing tonsils, a uterus, a kidney, fallopian tubes, a gall bladder, and eight feet of my small intestine.

My body still works just fine without those parts. However, sometimes when the parts don't work properly anymore, the body still needs those particular parts in order to function correctly.

The body is not like an automobile where you can go to the junk yard and pick out a few used parts to replace the defective ones. There can be biological replacements, like kidneys, lungs, hearts, etc. but sometimes there is no biological part available.

In those cases, parts need to be manufactured.

Full Dentures

For example, when my teeth failed to work properly, they needed to be replaced, but teeth are not something you can get on a list to wait for a biological replacement, like you can for a kidney or any of the other parts mentioned above.

Both my parents had full dentures. In fact, my Father had all his teeth replaced when he was a young man in the Navy. I'm not sure when Mom had hers replaced, but I do know that she wore dentures all through my teen and adult years.

It came to no surprise when, at age 50, I had to have all my teeth replaced. I had one of my front teeth capped with a gold cap when I was a teenager. The cap did not cover the entire front of the tooth, but it did cover the back and sides.

I had lots of problems with my teeth for most of my adult life. I am sure that some of it was my fault, I didn't always take the best care of my teeth, especially when I was younger, but I do believe there may be some genetics at work here as well.

My younger brother, Kelly (RIP), had full dentures the last 15 or 20 years of his life and my daughter, Amy, has had full dentures since she was in her late 30s. Bad teeth just seem to run in our family.

I have had dentures for the past 20 years and it just seems normal to me now that I put them in a cup on the bathroom counter at night. Someone once asked me if I took my shoes off when I went to bed.

I responded, "Of course."

She then said, "So I assume you also take your dentures off when you go to bed." That makes sense to me. I do know some people who only take their dentures off to clean them, but put them right back on and leave them on when they sleep.

Whatever choice a denture wearer makes, the point is that we need our teeth. Even if they wear out or fall out, they should be replaced. We can live perfectly normal lives with replaced teeth, just as we can with some of our other defective parts replaced.

Right Knee Replacement

I mentioned earlier that I tore the cartilage in both my knees when I was playing with a frisbee in the Arizona desert. That happened in the late 1980s, while I was in college in Missoula, Montana, and on Winter Break visiting my parents in Arizona.

When I returned to Missoula, I met with an orthopedic surgeon who recommended surgery to remove the torn cartilage. There was nothing replacing the removed cartilage, just space between the bones in both my knees.

In November of 2001, I was walking through the department at my work when my left knee collapsed and I fell down, striking a filing cabinet with my right arm. I had a spiral fracture of my arm as a result of my knee giving out.

That wasn't the first time my knee failed me and caused me to fall down. I once fell down the stairs in my house, blackening both my eyes. Another time I was walking across the parking lot at the hospital after visiting my mom, who was a patient on the telemetry (heart monitoring) ward.

I was getting tired of having to explain black eyes and bruises caused by me falling down. Since the break on my right arm was in the upper arm, the doctors could not put a cast on it, and I ended up wearing a sling for about nine months.

My orthopedic doctor x-rayed my knees when I told him how the accident happened. His first comment was "You had the cartilage removed about 20 years ago, right?" When I confirmed that yes, that was the case, he said they no longer removed cartilage when it was torn. It caused too many problems in the future, which was what I was now facing. The procedure now is to repair the cartilage whenever possible.

The joint was severely damaged because I had been walking on it without any cartilage between the upper and lower bones. They were out of alignment and rubbing bone-on-bone when I walked. He recommended knee replacement, although he did say that the new knee would likely need to be either replaced or revised in about 15 years.

I had to wait until my arm was completely healed before he would operate on my knee. My last day of wearing the sling was on a Friday in July 2002, and I had my right knee replaced the following Monday.

Recovery was not easy, and the whole process was quite painful. I had to put my right leg into a device that would flex it up and down several times a day. The only way I could use the device was with me lying down in my bed.

That went on for a couple weeks, then I started physical therapy at a local facility. This meant I had to get a ride to the facility and use a walker to get to the therapy room. This was my first experience using a walker.

There was also a cooler type of device with a tube running out of the ice packed inside to a pad that I was to keep on my knee while I was resting. It was cold, messy, and complicated.

Left Knee Replacement

My doctor wanted me to have the left knee replaced as well, but said I could wait six months or so as it was not as badly damaged as the left one.

I waited 15 years. By then my weight was spiraling out of control and my left knee was in terrible shape. I went to an orthopedic doctor in Arizona, but he did not want to do surgery until I got clearance from a cardiologist. Interestingly, he reported that my left knee replacement was still holding up quite well and I would not need to have it revised, even though it had been 15 years.

I had never been to a cardiologist, so I pulled out the phone book and found one close by. A few weeks later I was in the office, hooked up to a heart monitor and waiting for the nurse to start a stress test.

The nurse could not find a pulse. I was awake and talking to her, but my pulse rate had dropped significantly and when she looked at the computer readout of the leads attached to my chest, she said I was in second degree heart block.

That sounded pretty scary, but I felt fine. Needless to say, the cardiologist did not clear me for knee surgery, but did send me to the hospital to have a pacemaker installed. More about that later.

That was in September 2015. I put my house on the market the next spring and moved to Texas, where I started the process again to have my left knee replaced. I had been using a walker for some time and was tired of having to drag it around wherever I went.

In Texas I met with a lot of resistance from the orthopedic community. I saw three different doctors and all three of them refused to do the knee replacement because of my weight. They said the risk of infection was too great because I was so heavy. That is when I almost gave up as I mentioned before.

However, I did have one last doctor I wanted to see. I had heard that he did not care about how much the patient weighed, he just cared about helping them to walk normally again. It was early August 2016 by now and my knee was very painful.

When I saw Dr. Emerson, he looked at my x-rays and said: "You need to lose weight."

Oh, no, I thought, here it comes again. "Yes, I know that, but. . ."

He interrupted me, "But you can't walk. You can't exercise. You will never lose weight if you can't walk or exercise properly."

"That's true."

"So, here is what I will do. I will replace your knee if you will promise me that you will lose weight."

I agreed and we set a date for the surgery. Unfortunately, he was a terribly busy doctor and the next available date was in February 2017. I booked that date and went home.

The next week I met with Dr. Ayoola at the weight loss clinic and arranged to have the surgery. Again, I was forced to wait as the only opening Dr. Ayoola had on his schedule was in late March 2017.

In early December I received a call from Dr. Emerson's orthopedic office. They had an opening later that month; did I want it? Of course, I said yes, and I went into the hospital on December 13, 2016, and had my left knee replaced.

The recovery this time was a piece of cake compared to the surgery 15 years prior. No odd devices to go home with, no laying around in bed all the time with ice water flowing through a tube to a mat on my knee. They did send a physical therapist to my home three times a week and after each session I used an ice pack on my knee for 20 minutes or so.

Within a couple weeks I was walking fine. I no longer needed the walker and could get around with no assistance. I was still grossly overweight, however.

Repaired Parts

So far, I have talked about surgery to remove dysfunctional parts and surgery to replace parts. There is also surgery to repair parts. Sometimes when bones are severely broken, surgery is required to put them back together. In other instances, surgery can be done to fix broken parts or parts that have worn out or just don't work right anymore.

I have had to have a few of my parts repaired. Parts don't come with a warrantee, so when they stop working or get broken, they need to be fixed or replaced. I am fortunate in that I have had relatively good health insurance, but not everyone does.

Repairing parts can get quite expensive, and I'm sure there are many out there who cannot afford to undergo the proper treatments for repair or replacement of their parts. It is not easy to live with defective parts, just as it is not easy to drive a car with defective parts, but that is a discussion for another day.

Carpal Tunnel Syndrome

I have spent hours every day since I graduated from the University of Montana in 1986 working on the computer. Carpal Tunnel Syndrome is a common ailment among those of us who make repetitive movements with our hands.

In medical terms, *the carpal tunnel is a structure located in the wrist and includes the transverse carpal ligament and the carpal bones, which form the floor and the sides. The carpal tunnel contains nine flexor tendons and the median nerve. The median nerve is the main nerve of the forearm that supplies the forearm frontal structure. Its wrist branches supply the skin and the muscles of the thumb, index, middle, half of the ring finger, and the outer 2/3 of the palm. When the space inside the carpal tunnel narrows, the compression on the nerve ensues. Median nerve compression causes tingling and numbness in the palm, thumb, index, and ring fingers.* (Everything You Need to Know About Carpal Tunnel Syndrome, 2019)

What happened to me was not especially painful, but the numbness in my right hand was very concerning. I would be reading the morning paper (back when people read the paper in the morning) and my right hand would go numb. I could not even hold the page.

That enough was not serious enough to require surgery, but when the numbness started affecting my driving, it was time to see the doctor. I could not hold on to the steering wheel. My right hand and arm were completely useless. The doctor recommended the use of a brace for a while, but that did not change anything.

After lots of testing, he decided surgery was the answer. The scar starts at the bottom of the palm of my right hand and follows one of the natural so-called "lifelines" in my palm. Today the only way I can see the scar is if I hold my hand at a certain angle and squint. Even then, I am not sure if I am looking at a scar or a lifeline.

The surgery involved modifying the carpal tunnel in my right wrist to accommodate the median nerve and reduce the pressure on it. The repair worked perfectly, and I have had no issues since, despite still spending hours most days with repetitive movements on the computer keyboard.

After the doctor finished working on the inside of my wrist, he turned my hand over and removed a Bible cyst. You can read more about that modification in the Skin Cancer chapter. That scar is about an inch long and, although faded over the years, is still evident.

Hammer Toe (twice)

People in my family tend to have long toes, especially the second toe. When my kids were little, they used to tease me about my "finger toes." The second toe on each foot is longer than the first toe. When I was researching hammer toe, I discovered that, once again, I could check all the boxes for risk factors:

- ☐ **Age.** The risk of hammertoe and mallet toe increases with age. *(I had my first hammertoe surgery after I turned 50.)*

- ☐ **Sex.** Women are much more likely to develop hammertoe or mallet toe than are men. *(OK, another **benefit** of being female!)*

- ☐ **Toe length.** If your second toe is longer than your big toe, it is at higher risk of hammertoe or mallet toe. *(This is a family trait – finger toes!)*

- ☐ **Certain diseases.** Arthritis and diabetes might make you more prone to developing foot deformities. Heredity might also play a role. *(I do not have diabetes, but I do have arthritis – and of course, the genetic trait of long second toes makes this one true, too.)* (Mayo Foundation for Medical Education and Research, 2020)

The older I got, the more my toes became deformed. According to the Mayo Clinic website, a hammertoe is an abnormal bend in the middle joint of a toe. On my left foot, the second toe bent so far that I could not put on shoes. The middle joint pointed straight up, and the rest of the toe tried to crawl under my big toe.

I saw a podiatrist, who recommended surgery. The surgery involved straightening the toe joints out, and placing a pin through the bone from the end up to where the toe met my foot. For six weeks, I sported a bright yellow pinhead the size of a small marble on the end of my newly straightened toe. The pinhead was eventually removed, but the pin is still there. I can't bend that toe at all, but at least it is straight, and I can wear shoes.

On the other foot, the second toe simply bent itself sideways, getting under my big toe and causing a great deal of pain when I walked. I had that one straightened as well, but this time the doctor did not put a pin in it.

My toes still bend directions they shouldn't but they don't get under each other, they just look funny. I can walk with out issues.

Morton's Neuroma

People who have bunions, hammertoes, high arches or flatfeet are at higher risk of developing Morton's neuroma. Morton's neuroma is a painful condition that affects the ball of your foot, most commonly the area between your third and fourth toes. Morton's neuroma may feel as if you are standing on a pebble in your shoe or on a fold in your sock. (Mayo Foundation for Medical Education and Research, 2020)

This is a very painful condition, one I developed in my left foot about the same time my hammertoe was getting bothersome. Morton's neuroma involves a thickening of the tissue around one of the nerves leading to your toes. This can cause a sharp, burning pain in the ball of your foot. Your toes also may sting, burn or feel numb.

I felt as though there was a large marble in my foot. When the podiatrist straightened out the hammertoe, he also repaired the nerve in my foot, removing the neuroma.

I am now developing quite an impressive bunion on that foot, but will not have surgery on it.

A bunion occurs when the big toe starts to wander over toward the other toes causing a bump at the top joint. It can be painful when wearing tight shoes. I wear sandals and flip-flops a lot now. The bunion doesn't bother me.

Injured Parts

Sometimes our parts get injured. Injuries come in the form of simple cuts and bruises to broken bones or other, more severe injuries. Depending on severity, the injured parts can heal with no intervention from the medical field. More severe injured parts will need some kind of intervention, but once healed, the parts continue to do what they were meant to without being replaced or removed.

Bruises

A bruise is the result of blood leaking out of the capillaries (the small blood vessels that lie closest to the surface of your skin). When you hit something, or something hits you the pressure from the strike causes the capillaries to leak.

I know several people my age and older who seem to bruise easily. My Dad was always sporting large, purple bruises on his arms and legs. His skin became thinner the older he got. He was also taking blood thinners to control his blood flow and prevent blood clots.

A known side effect of blood thinners is bruising easily, meaning that Dad did not have to get hit or hit something in order for a bruise to form. Sometimes just a slight pinch or even a tap on the arm would leave a big purple mark.

I don't take blood thinners, and although my skin is thinning as I age, extensive bruising is not something that I suffer from. I do get a bruise on occasion, just like everyone else, but nothing like the bruising I have seen on other older people's arms.

The most bruising I have had to deal with is after an IV or blood draw. My veins tend to roll around or are very hard to find, so the lab techs typically have to dig around or poke me multiple times, resulting in some impressive bruises.

When I broke my arm, I ended up with spectacular bruises all down my right side. They were quite colorful as time went on, starting with a deep purple, moving into a lighter blue with red tinges, and finally turning yellow. In the end, the bruises were gone, and my skin was intact.

Broken Bones

As I mentioned before, I fell at work because my knee gave out as I was walking through my office. I struck my arm on a file cabinet, causing a spiral fracture. Fortunately, my broken arm was not a compound fracture and did not require surgery. It was, however, in the upper part of my arm and could not be put in a cast.

When I fell, my co-workers called 911, knowing I would need to go to the hospital. I remember that one of my staff members offered to ride to the hospital with me, but she did not ride in the back of the ambulance. She rode in the front, with the paramedics. Later, when I asked her why, she grinned, blushed, and asked, "Did you see them?"

For weeks after that incident, the female staff in my department thanked me for breaking my arm. Apparently, the firefighters and EMTs that answered the call were quite attractive. I had a good laugh about that.

The doctor put me in a splint for about nine months. It was my right arm, and I am right-handed. There was temporary nerve damage caused by the twisting arm bone and for a few weeks my right hand was limp.

I could not move it at all, so I had to learn to do things with my left hand and arm. I got to where I was quite good using the mouse on the left side of my computer instead of the right side, but when I was able to take the splint off, I went right back to using my right hand.

The splint was removed on a Friday in July, and I had my knee replaced the following Monday, a couple months after one of my granddaughters was born. She is 18 now and both my replaced knee and repaired broken arm are just fine.

A few years ago, I was diagnosed with Osteopenia, the precursor to Osteoporosis. This is fairly common as people get older, and women tend to suffer from it more than men. That diagnosis recently changed to Osteoporosis, a condition where the bones become more porous, increasing the risk of breaking.

According to the doctor, my bones are porous enough that if I do fall, I have a 25% risk of breaking a bone. The most common bone people break from Osteoporosis is the hip. I was told again to avoid things like rappelling off the side of mountains, sky diving, and motocross racing. Again! I never seem to catch a break in the extreme sports area – LOL. Basically, I just need to be careful and not put myself in a position where I risk falling.

Sometimes the disease progresses so much that patients will break bones without falling. I'm not there and I don't plan on getting there. I take medication, one pill a week, to slow down or even stop progression of the condition.

I have only had one broken bone in my life – the one I mentioned at the beginning of this chapter – and I plan on keeping it that way.

Sick Parts

One thing I can say about illness is that I have never really been sick. At least I don't believe I have been sick. My family and even a few of my doctors may disagree with that assessment.

I have never had the flu (I didn't start getting an annual flu shot until I turned 65). I have had a cough or a sore throat that lasted maybe 24 hours.

It is now early Spring, 2020, and I cannot write this section without mentioning the Corona Virus, or COVID-19. As of this writing, nobody I know, family or friend, has the virus. We are all self-quarantining, working from home, and wondering why in the world people are hoarding toilet paper.

Every day the news is filled with dire predictions, unsettling statistics about the increase in the number of positive test results, and more deaths due to this horrendous pandemic. The general consensus from the medical field is that it will get worse before it gets better, with a peak in cases coming in the next few weeks.

It is highly possible that someone I know, even myself, could come in contact with the virus. I am in what is considered to be a high-risk group because of my age, but I continue to believe that I, along with my family and friends, will be fine. I do not consider myself to have any underlying medical conditions, I practice social distancing, and I feel fine, as usual.

I don't remember taking a sick day from work because I was actually sick. I do remember taking a sick day on occasion just because I didn't feel like going to work, but I don't remember any prolonged illness. I did have the measles and chickenpox when I was a kid, but don't remember being sick at all.

That is, until I had cancer. Even then, I was never really sick. I completed my cancer treatment well before the onset of the Corona Virus, so do not consider it to be an underlying medical condition, putting me in an even higher risk group.

Anal Cancer

I had not had a colonoscopy since I turned 50, which is when the medical profession at that time recommended starting that examination process. They also recommended that the test be repeated every five years. I waited more than 15 years for my second colonoscopy. Now the recommendation is to start having periodic colonoscopies at age 45.

I was planning a trip to Europe in late June 2018, with my family. We were going to all meet in Croatia to celebrate my son's 50th birthday. He was living in Germany with his family and a trip to Croatia for him was like us taking a trip to Florida or California for vacation.

My daughter, Roni, and her husband and daughter were going to Rome for a week before the Croatia trip, so I planned an initial rendezvous in Venice. I would be traveling from Dallas to Italy with my granddaughter, Darrah, and her family. It was going to be a long flight.

We would spend a couple days in Venice before taking a five-hour ferry trip across the Adriatic Sea to Croatia.

I had been uncomfortable sitting because of what I assumed were hemorrhoids, and knew I was way overdue for a colonoscopy. I made an appointment and visited a colon-rectal surgeon the first week in April.

As I lay on my side so the doctor could examine me, I braced myself by putting my hand on the wall next to the examination table. I was a bit nervous in that vulnerable position, so I joked with the doctor, saying, "I bet you get a lot of fingerprints on this wall." Her response? "Mostly claw marks!" I knew right then I was going to like this doctor. She had a sense of humor.

Her next comment, however, made me pause for a minute. "Hmmm. I didn't expect to see that!" she said. I assumed she was just surprised by the size of what I thought was a hemorrhoid and thought no more about her comment until much later.

She left the room while I got dressed and I expected to see her nurse come in with instructions for the next steps. But the doctor came back in and said she wanted me to schedule a colonoscopy as soon as possible.

Well, that was the reason I was there, after all, so again I was not surprised. I wondered for a moment, however, why she did not mention any treatment options for the hemorrhoids. But I figured she would bring that up after the colonoscopy, which I had a few days later.

I was wrong. I did not have hemorrhoids. I had a tumor and a biopsy was ordered. We got the results a few days later: Malignant for Anal Cancer.

All I could think about was the trip to Europe – would I have to cancel it? The doctor referred me to North Texas Oncology Center. She said the treatment could be as long as six months, but was not sure about that. She also said that, although Anal Cancer was fairly rare, if a person could choose the cancer they get, Anal Cancer was the one to get because it is relatively easy to cure.

I have to admit right here that I still did not believe I had cancer. I did not feel any different than I had before the colonoscopy. I was under the mistaken impression that cancer meant life was over, or soon would be. People with cancer looked and felt sick. They were bald, they spent their days in bed, waiting to die, and then they died. That was not me. I felt just fine. I couldn't possibly have cancer.

I made an appointment at the Cancer Center, however, just to appease those around me. I didn't think I needed to go, but I went. I was scheduled for a PET scan before I met with two doctors, one a hematologist and one a radiologist.

The PET scan confirmed the cancer diagnosis and pinpointed the location of the tumor. It had not spread, and

I was told I had Stage 3 Anal Cancer. I had to believe the doctors now.

The radiologist was a friendly, open, kind man. He brought a cup of tea to the exam room. His little dog accompanied him around the radiology department. He told me I would have a radiation treatment every weekday for six weeks. Because of the targeted area for the radiation therapy (the tumor on my anus) there would be some discomfort in the future.

Well, discomfort is not the word he used. He said, *"I'm going to set off a roman candle in you're a$$!"* He wasn't kidding. Anal cancer may be the easiest to cure, but it has to be one of the more painful ones. I met with the radiation nurses, who gave me my first (and only) tattoos. I now have four tiny blue dots etched into my skin as markers for the radiation machine. One on each hip, one below my belly button, and one a few inches lower.

The radiation itself is not painful. I went to the clinic every weekday morning for the next six weeks and spent about five minutes on the table under the machine, then went home. No pain.

The pain came later; it was from the accumulation of radiation treatments. The tissues surrounding the tumor were burned. Once treatment was over, it took several months to be completely healed.

The hematologist was a good doctor, but more clinically oriented than the radiologist. He did not bring tea and he was not followed around by a puppy. But he was friendly enough, and knowledgeable about cancer and its effect on the body.

He ordered a round of chemo in the lab the first day of radiation treatment, followed by four days of wearing a fanny pack with a bag of chemo in the pouch. The bag was attached to a pump and a tube that was attached to a port in my right upper chest.

The port had been installed the previous week. It was a small device inserted just under my skin, with a direct line to a vein in my neck. The pump delivered small doses of chemo through the tube into my blood stream consistently for four days. I felt nothing as a result of this treatment. I did not get sick, I did not lose my hair, and I only knew I was being treated because of the constant buzzing of the chemo pump and the tube attached to my chest.

At the end of the six weeks of radiation, I had another hour or so of chemo infused through my port. This took place in the infusion room at the Cancer Center. I had no side effects.

In fact, the ONLY side effects I had during the whole time were the acute burning sensation in my nether regions after the radiation treatments ended.

The treatment ended on June 7, 2018 and I attended the first of several events I had already planned over the summer. On June 9, I went to the DFWCON writer's conference and spent three days with writers and editors. I spent the evenings in my hotel room, however, not participating in the dinners and after dinner events. I was tired and needed to conserve my strength for the daytime activities.

I also went to Venice on June 20, then on to Croatia and Germany before returning home on July 12. The aftereffects of the chemo made me tired, but I had a great time visiting with my family and did not think about cancer.

I specifically remember one morning in Venice. We were staying in an apartment on the fourth floor of an old building fronting a small square. There was no elevator in the building, making navigating the stairs very difficult for me. I had to rest after climbing just a few steps, so it took around 30 minutes to get to the apartment.

The day after we arrived in Venice, my family wanted to explore the city. I knew that walking around the area, filled with steps, bridges, and no cars, would be difficult for me, so I decided to stay back in the square below our apartment.

There were shops and small restaurants in the square, plenty of things to keep me occupied. I started out by sitting in the patio just outside a restaurant, sampling a typical Italian breakfast. People watching is a great way to learn about an area.

My family stopped by my table on their way to explore the city, wondering if I would be OK all by myself. Of course, I would be just fine, I told them. I was, after all, in Venice! It was about two weeks since I had completed the cancer treatment and the worst of the radiation aftereffects hadn't kicked in yet.

It took some work on my part, but I never gave up. I always thought of the cancer as simply a bump in the road. Something I had to take care of before I embarked on my planned summer. My apartment lease was up the first of May and I moved in with my daughter for the summer. My moving in with her eased her mind because of the cancer treatment I had started, and it gave me a bit of a financial break, seeing as I was not going to be working all summer. She did try to convince me to at least skip the Venice part of the trip because of all the walking and stair climbing I would have to do during those three days. I said no.

On the 21st of June I spent most of the day sitting in a café on the plaza below the Air BnB rooms we had rented on the fourth floor of an old, beautiful building in Venice. The walk the day before was hard. I had to crawl up the last two flights of stairs to get to the rooms. I was tired and weak from the chemo and radiation. But I was in Venice!

Sitting in the café that day while my family explored Venice was wonderful. I watched people, talked to other tourists, met a cancer doctor (of all things) from Great Britain who was attending a conference in Venice, and had a delightful conversation with 60-year old newlyweds from Key West, Florida who were starting the next phase of their lives in Venice. My daughter felt bad that I was unable to tour the city with them, but you know what? I didn't feel bad at all. I was, after all, in Venice! The entire summer, including the cancer sidebar in the Spring was timed perfectly with angels looking over my shoulder the entire time.

Having cancer in the spring did not slow me down at all. In fact, I still have problems believing I actually had cancer. The port in my right shoulder was removed in December 2018, taking away the last "proof" that something happened that spring.

I am on the five-year plan now. Apparently, the medical profession maintains that a person who had cancer is in *remission* until declared cancer-free. They will not declare a patient cancer free for a minimum of five years without a recurrence.

When I was first diagnosed, I was told I would lose my hair from the chemo treatments. I had heard that when cancer patients re-grew their hair after losing it, it came back with a different texture. My hair has always been very thick and straight. I decided that if I did lose my hair, I wanted it to come back curly and purple. As it happened, my hair thinned out a bit, but did not completely go away. When it thickened up again, there was a bit of curl in it that had not been there before, but it was still white and grey (it was red when I was younger).

I promptly died my hair lavender. I have kept it lavender since the fall of 2018. Only the whiter parts of it hold onto the color, but that's OK. Everyone I see likes it, I like it, and I really like being lavender. It reminds me of a favorite poem:

"Warning" by Jenny Joseph

When I am an old woman I shall wear purple,
With a red hat which doesn't go, and doesn't suit me.
And I shall spend my pension on brandy and summer gloves,
And satin sandals, and say we've no money for butter.

I shall sit down on the pavement when I'm tired,
And gobble up samples in shops and press alarm bells,
And run my stick along the public railings
And make up for the sobriety of my youth.

I shall go out in my slippers in the rain,
And pick flowers in other people's gardens,
And learn to spit.

You can wear terrible shirts and grow more fat,
And eat three pounds of sausages at a go,
Or only bread and pickle for a week,
And hoard pens and pencils and beermats and things in boxes.

But now we must have clothes that keep us dry,
And pay our rent and not swear in the street,
And set a good example for the children.
We must have friends to dinner and read the papers.

But maybe I ought to practice a little now?
So people who know me are not too shocked and surprised,
When suddenly I am old, and start to wear purple.
(Joseph, 2017)

I have had a CT scan every six months since I completed treatment in June 2018. I am cancer-free, according to me. I don't particularly like the word *remission*, as I believe it implies it is coming back. I do not believe it is coming back. My next check-up is the end of June 2020.

Skin Cancer

I have a memory from when I was around four or maybe five of standing on the toilet after my bath and my mother slathering my entire body with mineral oil. My skin has always been incredibly dry. I remember the big bottle of clear, odorless oil Mom used to keep me from drying out. I think it just made me very slippery.

I did suffer from eczema when I was a pre-teen. I had big red, itchy patches of skin in the inner folds of my elbows. They were worse in the summer. I outgrew that, but still as an adult suffer from very dry skin and scalp.

However, I have had a problem with skin cancer as an adult. According to *"Dr. Google"* the people most at risk for developing skin cancer have the following characteristics:

- Freckles
- Fair skin tone
- Skin that does not tan or that tans poorly
- Skin that burns easily
- Light colored eyes, such as green or blue
- Naturally red or blonde hair (the former carries more risk than the latter)

While there are a lot more risk factors involved, including severe sunburns as a youth, exposure to UV rays in tanning beds, etc., I can certainly check all the boxes on the list above. My dermatologist, as I mentioned before, said I was very good at growing things on my skin, like basil cell cancers and benign cysts. I also tend grow internal cysts like the ones on my kidneys.

I would like to be known as being good at other things! Not things like skin cancer and cysts. I have had five basil cell carcinomas (the most common, and least dangerous skin cancer) removed from my body. One on my belly, one on the back of my neck one on my right cheek and one near each eye.

A common method of treating skin cancer is called Mohs surgery, named after Dr. Frederick Mohs, who developed the procedure in 1938. During Mohs surgery the doctor removes thin layers of the skin containing cancerous cells. One by one, she removes the layers then examines them for cancerous cells. The patient waits while the layers are being examined. If the edges of the removed tissue still contain cancer cells, the doctor goes in and removes more tissue. This is repeated until there are no longer cancerous cells in the layers. Once the surgery is complete, a plastic surgeon closes the wound. (Felson, Sabrina MD, 2019)

The first time I had Mohs surgery (I had a pencil eraser sized basil cell cancer at the inside corner of my left eye) the doctor had to make two passes to get it all. The incision ran along the edge of my nose up into my forehead. After surgery, a plastic surgeon closed up the wound. He was very good, and there is no discernable scar, although the stitches ran all the way up my nose to about an inch above my right eyebrow.

The second time I had Mohs, the doctor only needed to make one pass to get all the cancer. The same plastic surgeon stitched up a chevron shaped incision running below my eye to a point near my nose, then back down toward the center of my cheek.

I recently had a follow-up visit with that plastic surgeon. He was quite pleased at my progress; the scar barely shows. He said that this one would take longer, but eventually the scar would disappear. We discussed my propensity to grow basil cell carcinomas and he recommended I see my regular dermatologist frequently to make sure I am not growing more of them. His words: *"We're done with this one, but this is not the last time I will be seeing you!"*

I may have imagined him letting out an evil laugh (Bua-ha-ha) as he left the examination room.

As for benign Pilar cysts, I tend to grow those on my scalp. Pilar cysts are noncancerous, flesh-colored, round bumps that develop under the surface of the skin. This type of cyst is caused by protein buildup in a hair follicle.

They present as raised bumps that are not painful, but they interfered with brushing my hair. I have had four of them removed, three just this past year.

I did have a cyst on the back of my right wrist several years ago; it was a ganglion cyst, sometimes called a *Book cyst,* (sometimes called a *Bible cyst.)* A ganglion cyst is a round, fluid-filled lump of tissue that usually appears along tendons or joints, especially in the hands, wrists, ankles, and feet.

The reason it was called a *Book* or *Bible cyst,* according to the doctor, was because many years ago, they were treated by smashing them with a heavy book, like the Bible. I had mine removed when I had carpal tunnel surgery.

Medications

After I had surgery to remove the eight feet of dead bowel from my small intestine, I was sent home from the hospital with a home health nurse. I was assigned a physical therapist at the same time. Both of these medical professionals came to my home to assess my condition and make sure I was taking my medications as well as getting the proper exercise.

The nurse asked me for a list of my medications so he could make sure his records were accurate. I told him about the pill I was taking for hypothyroidism and the one I took for high cholesterol. He asked for the rest. There were no others. He was surprised and said that usually when he asked for medication lists from senior citizens, they presented him with a whole tub full of prescription bottles.

As of today, nine months after that encounter, I am taking three medications; the two I mentioned and the weekly pill I now take for osteoporosis. I do take some vitamin, iron, and calcium supplements as well.

Before I lost all the weight, I was on three different high blood pressure meds as well as a higher dose of the cholesterol medication. My cardiologist told me at my last visit that, depending on results from my blood work in June this year, she would probably stop the cholesterol medication. I haven't needed the blood pressure meds for nearly two years now.

Extra Parts Added

Even though we are born with lots of parts, sometimes there are not enough parts to do the job. Especially as we get older. Our parts may work well for a while then, as time goes by, they get worn out or simply cease to work properly.

That is when the doctors come in and add parts to enhance the performance of the existing parts. I have seen, as I am sure you have, small children, even babies, wearing glasses. Their eyes did not work well from the start, others don't start wearing glasses or contacts until much later in life.

These extra parts are not meant to replace the malfunctioning parts, but are meant to help them work better. There are lots of kinds of extra parts, some are simply added externally and can be removed easily by the wearer. Crutches, glasses, contacts, orthopedic shoes, etc. are not permanently attached.

Extra parts can also be surgically installed, providing permanent enhancement or help for the malfunctioning parts. Pacemakers, heart monitors, colostomy bags, and implanted cancer ports are surgically attached on or inside the body. These parts can be either permanent or temporary, depending on the reason for installing the part.

I've been fortunate in that I have not had to have many of my working parts enhanced by the insertion of extra parts, but there have been a few.

Pacemaker

In late 2015, after returning home to Arizona from my granddaughter's destination wedding in Jamaica, I decided it was time to get my left knee replaced. The only way I could walk was with a walker. The orthopedic surgeon agreed to do the surgery, but said I needed cardiac clearance first.

As related before, I found a cardiologist and went in for a stress test. The nurses could not find a pulse (a recurring issue with me) even though I was sitting up and talking. I was hooked up to a computer that showed my pulse rate down to around 29 (60 is considered normal) which is why the nurse could not find it. The computer screen also showed that I was experiencing second degree heart block.

According to the ACLS-Algorithms website, second degree heart block is defined as: *Second degree heart block Type 2, which is also called Mobitz II or Hay, is a disease of the electrical conduction system of the heart. Second-degree AV block (Type 2) is almost always a disease of the distal conduction system located in the ventricular portion of the myocardium.* ((ACLS) Advanced Cardiac Life Support, 2020)

The website goes on to say, "*Second-degree AV block (Type 2) should be treated with immediate transcutaneous pacing or transvenous pacing because there is risk that electrical impulses will not be able to reach the ventricles and produce ventricular contraction."*

What that meant was my stress test was cancelled, the nurse called the cardiologist ("plumber") who recommended an electrophysiologist ("electrician"). Based on the information they had at hand, including the computer printouts, the lack of a discernable pulse, the doctor recommended I be taken immediately to the adjacent hospital for the insertion of a pacemaker.

I want to be clear at this point in the narrative. I felt fine. I was breathing, walking, talking, and exhibited no symptoms of heart issues. That's not to say I wasn't in trouble, but I never would have gone to the cardiologist in the first place if I wasn't looking for cardiac clearance for my knee surgery. Who knows what would have happened if I had not gone in that day?

I had evidently been experiencing the low pulse rate off and on for some time without knowing it. I do remember feeling lightheaded on several occasions, but they were always at night while I was in bed. I would turn over and feel as though I was going to faint. The feeling would pass, and I would not think about it again.

Evidently those near fainting spells were when my heart rate was at its lowest.

I spent the night in the hospital and had a pacemaker inserted just under the skin on the inside of my left shoulder the next morning. It was Thursday and I had a book signing scheduled at a local bookstore on Saturday. I wanted to get out of the hospital in time to make it to the signing.

I went home on Friday and was able to make the signing on Saturday with no problem. I sometimes forget the pacemaker is still there. In fact, I am surprised sometimes when I feel it in the pouch under my skin, then I remember. It has been five years since that day, and I will have the pacemaker for the rest of my life. The battery will need to be replaced in another five years.

I did have one issue with it. When it was originally installed, I was near my highest weight and there was a lot of fatty tissue in the area where the pacemaker was placed. The procedure is to create a pouch under the skin just under the collar bone, place the pacemaker (about the size of a kidney-shaped silver dollar) in the pouch, an attach the leads to it.

The leads are wires going to the heart. When the heart rate slows down, the pacemaker creates an electrical pulse that goes through the leads and stimulates the heart. That's the best way I can describe it in non-medical terms. I cannot feel the pulses and have no idea when the pacer is resting or pacing.

The problem I had was when I lost so much weight a few years after having the pacemaker installed. It started just "floating" around in my upper chest area. There was nothing to hook it too when the fatty tissue disappeared. I would turn on my side and it would flip sideways – sticking out perpendicular to my body. It didn't hurt, but it was concerning.

I went back to the heart electrician, who chuckled at my dilemma a bit, then scheduled me for a quick "realignment" surgery. She explained she would place my pacemaker in a small pouch made of a material that would eventually dissolve. She called it a "kangaroo pouch." She would then attach the pouch to the muscles in my chest, stabilizing the pacemaker.

That was two years ago, and it seems to be fine now. I can feel the pacemaker under my skin, but it does not dance around. Most of the time I forget it is there. It does make for an interesting time at airports, however. I have to go through the full body scanner because of the metal in my body.

I have to have a pat-down every time I go through the scanner, both because of the pacemaker and my two artificial knees. I light up the machine like a Christmas tree every time! I call the pat-down my free, government massage.

Cancer Port

When I was diagnosed with cancer and told I would be undergoing chemotherapy treatment, one of my first concerns was having to be poked with a needle hooked up to the chemo bag. My veins are not exactly easy to find, sometimes causing lots of bruising. They either roll or are very deep. Many times, the nurses have to call in someone else just to get an IV started.

Cancer patients often have to go through this procedure multiple times during the course of their treatment, but there is a solution: The Cancer Port. This is a small device implanted just under the skin, usually in the front of the shoulder. The device has a line that is threaded through the patient's body to a vein in the neck, creating access for IVs, chemotherapy, and saline solutions.

It is a temporary solution, typically removed once treatment is completed. My cancer port was implanted in May 2018 and removed the following December. I completed cancer treatment in June, but they wanted to make sure the cancer was gone before removing the port.

My pacemaker is in my left shoulder, so the port went into my right shoulder. It was placed while I was under general anesthesia, but they removed it with just a local, so I was awake as they took it out. I could feel it, it was a small button-shaped lump in my shoulder. I could see the tube threading from it to my neck – looked like a wire under my skin.

Having something like this added to my body was not what I expected, but it sure made it easy for the nurses to administer the chemo. I was dehydrated a couple times during treatment, so they were able to give me saline solution infusions with no problem through the port. When I went in for my follow-up PET scans, the technician was able to insert the IV needle in the port to inject the solution needed for the scan.

When I ended up in the ER a year and a half later, it would have been nice to still have the port – hours could have been saved trying to hook up IVs!

Glasses

Unlike the pacemaker and cancer port, glasses are external added parts. They require no surgery and can be considered as temporary. Sometimes glasses are needed from infancy on, but in my case, I didn't need glasses until shortly before I turned 20.

My eyes have steadily gotten weaker, and my glasses stronger, until now, at 70 I cannot read a book, the computer screen, or the dashboard in the car without my glasses. I can, however, see the television screen, a movie screen, etc. with no problem.

I laughed when I went to the theater with a friend of mine who also wears glasses. Once we were settled in our seats, she put on her glasses and I took mine off. I am what is considered farsighted. Farsightedness (hyperopia) is a common vision condition in which you can see distant objects clearly, but objects nearby may be blurry.

My friend, on the other hand, is nearsighted. Nearsightedness (myopia) is a common vision condition in which you can see objects near to you clearly, but objects farther away are blurry. It occurs when the shape of your eye causes light rays to bend (refract) incorrectly, focusing images in front of your retina instead of on your retina.

Issues with vision tend to run in families. Most of my family members have some issues, some wear glasses to read, some to see distances. Some of them only wear glasses sometimes. I have never worn contacts, although members of my family have.

Glasses are a necessary item in my collection of "parts," enhancing my vision so I can perform my daily tasks. I can take them off when I want, change them, clean them, etc. They do not replace any of my existing parts, but without them I could not see to write this book.

Where do the "Parts" go?

My friend, Shelia Embry, likes to joke about *"leaving body parts all over the country.... tonsils in Kentucky, a uterus in Virginia, a thyroid in DC, a gallbladder and 1/3 stomach in New York....ugh...."* I've done something similar: tonsils and uterus in Billings, Montana, a fallopian tube and ovary in Las Vegas, Nevada, a kidney in Missoula, Montana, a knee in Phoenix, Arizona, another knee, gallbladder and eight feet of a small intestine in Dallas, Texas.

It sounds like the parts were just discarded, tossed out with the trash, or dropped on the side of the road. That's obviously not the case, but where do they go? What happens to all these "parts?" They are considered biohazard waste and cannot, by law, just be tossed in the trash.

According to the United Medical Industries website, there are five types of biohazardous waste.

1. Solid Biohazardous Waste
2. Liquid Biohazardous Waste
3. Sharp Biohazardous Waste
4. Pathological Biohazardous Waste
5. Microbiological Waste (UMI Biomedical, 2018)

This book is primarily about type #4. **Pathological Biohazardous Waste**. *Pathological waste includes any removed animal or human organs, tissues, and body parts. Any of these may contain infectious agents.*

Waste materials from a biopsy procedure fall into this category. Another example is anatomical parts that personnel removed during autopsies or surgeries.

How to Dispose of Pathological Waste

Healthcare personnel should double-bag pathological waste to prevent leaks. Personnel should then store it in a secondary container as they would liquid waste.

From there, they dispose of it by incineration or other chemical treatment. Autoclaving is not appropriate for pathological waste.
(UMI Biomedical, 2018)

Basically, what happens is the "parts" are reserved for study, protected from contamination, and, once they are no longer useful, are incinerated or disposed of using chemical treatments.

Epilogue

If you read all the way through this, you know just about everything medically about me. So, if or when we get together in the future, whether in person or virtually, let's talk about who we are, what we have accomplished, our families and important events, but not about our broken bones, surgeries, illnesses, or any of that stuff. We ALL have gone through medical situations, and come out on the other side to go on and do whatever we were meant to do.

One of my friends thought that the woman in the red turban that came to me in the hospital was there to tell me it wasn't my time. I still had things to do. I believe she was right. The medical issues were hiccups along the way. They didn't stop me, and your medical trials won't stop you if you don't let them.

Carry on.

References

(ACLS) Advanced Cardiac Life Support. (2020). Retrieved from ACLS-Algorithms: https://acls-algorithms.com/rhythms/second-degree-heart-block-type-2/

Biggs, M. (2020, February 10). *Texas Health Resources*. Retrieved from Are You a Well Being?: https://areyouawellbeing.texashealth.org/writer-prepares-to-share-her-miraculous-health-story-on-paper/

Embry, S. (2020). *At the Right Time.* janiewrites.

Everything You Need to Know About Carpal Tunnel Syndrome. (2019). Retrieved from Beta Healthy: https://betahealthy.com/everything-you-need-to-know-about-carpal-tunnel-syndrome-symptomssignscauses-risk-factors-and-treatments/?utm_source=bing&utm_medium=cpc&utm_campaign=Carpal%20Tunnel%20Syndrome&utm_term=what%20is%20carpal%20tunnel&utm_content=Carpa

Felson, Sabrina MD. (2019, October 13). *What is Mohs Surgery?* Retrieved from WebMD: https://www.webmd.com/melanoma-skin-cancer/mohs-surgery#1

Joseph, J. (2017, April 19). *James Milson - Writing & Things*. Retrieved from "Warning" Poem by Jenny Joseph: https://jamesmilson.com/2017/04/19/warning-poem-by-jenny-joseph-when-i-grow-old-i-shall-wear-purple/

Looking on the Bright Side: The Health Benefits of Positive Thinking. (2020, February 21). Retrieved from Guardian: https://www.guardiandirect.com/resources/articles/looking-bright-side-health-benefits-positive-thinking

Mayo Foundation for Medical Education and Research. (2020). *Hammertoe and Mallet Toe*. Retrieved from Mayo Clinic: https://www.mayoclinic.org/diseases-conditions/hammertoe-and-mallet-toe/symptoms-causes/syc-20350839

Mayo Foundation for Medical Education and Research. (2020). *Morton's neuroma*. Retrieved from Mayo Clinic: https://www.mayoclinic.org/diseases-conditions/mortons-neuroma/symptoms-causes/syc-20351935

Pullman, A. (2018). *I Want My Body Back*. Annadale, Virginia: JanieWrites.

Pullman, A. (2018). *Self Esteem and Your Unique Style*. Annadale, VA: JanieWrites.

UMI Biomedical. (2018, January 24). *UMI*. Retrieved from 5 Types of Biohazardous Waste (and How to Dispose): https://umibiomedical.com/5-types-biohazardous-waste/